Whose Wedding Is It Anyway?

A play

Margaret Bower

Samuel French — London
New York — Toronto — Hollywood

CHARACTERS

Mrs Aldridge
Myra
Mavis
Mother
Aunty Flo

Time — the present

AUTHOR'S NOTE

Mrs Aldridge wears her everyday clothes, but has made a pretence of going to the wedding by wearing a hat.

Myra wears good quality but rather dull clothes and hat.

Mavis is dressed more extravagantly, but still in the best of taste. Her hat can be either large and flamboyant or merely a wisp of veiling.

Mother wears dressing- gown and slippers for her first entrance. Later her costume is outrageously glamourous — trousers, coloured silk shirt, expensive trainers and a large sun hat. She carries a large handbag or a small travel bag.

Aunty Flo wears her ordinary coat or mac.

Whose Wedding Is It Anyway?

The scene is mother's sitting room. There is a small settee DL and two easy chairs R. Small tables DR and DL. UC is a sideboard or table with a sherry bottle and glasses on it, and a mirror above. Other furniture as desired to make the room look comfortable and lived in. There is an entrance from the front door and stairs L and an entrance from the kitchen R

As the CURTAIN *rises Mrs Aldridge is seated DR draining the last dregs from a glass of sherry. She even wipes her finger round the glass and sucks it*

Myra enters L

Myra Sorry to have abandoned you, Mrs Aldridge. I was just checking if Mother needed any help. Perhaps you would like another glass of sherry while we are waiting?

Mrs Aldridge I don't mind if I do.

Myra Perhaps I will have one myself. I feel rather in need of it.

Mrs Aldridge Nervous are you?

Myra Yes, I am rather. I can't think why at my age. (*She pours the sherries at the sideboard then sits on the settee DL*)

Mrs Aldridge Weddings are like that. I remember mine — my first that is. Well, I was only seventeen and as innocent as a new born babe. Not like the youngsters these days. If I'd known then what I know now! We went to Brighton for our honeymoon, just for the weekend you know, and when we got to the hotel; well it weren't a proper hotel, just a B and B, but ever so nice, well, my Lenny said to me, you go up to the room Lil and I'll follow you in a minute. Well, I went up and do you know ...

Myra (*getting up; going to the sideboard*) Thank you, Mrs Aldridge I don't think I want to hear ...

Mrs Aldridge (*following her*) When I got to the room, you'll never believe this, there was this great big double bed and in the corner was a baby's cot — talk about embarrassed, I thought I'd die ...

The doorbell rings

Myra (*relieved*) Excuse me, Mrs Aldridge.

Myra exits L

Mrs Aldridge checks that Myra is safely out of the way, pours herself another drink and returns to her seat, the picture of innocence

Myra returns followed by Mavis

Come on in, Mavis. This is my sister Mrs Burton. Mavis, I don't suppose you have met Mrs Aldridge.

Mrs Aldridge How d'you do.

Mavis How do you do, Mrs Aldridge. (*She looks questioningly at Myra*)

Myra Mrs Aldridge is Mother's — um — housekeeper.

Mrs Aldridge Ooh, hark at her — housekeeper! I'm the lady what does, as they say.

Mavis I beg your pardon?

Mrs Aldridge Your mum's daily help.

Mavis Oh, I see. (*She sits on the settee* DL)

Mrs Aldridge Lovely lady your mum, I've been with her over five years now. Funny we've never met before. Don't you ever come and see your mum?

Myra (*sitting on the easy chair* UR) Mavis and her husband live in Newcastle. They don't get down this way very often.

Mrs Aldridge What, not in five years!

Mavis Yes of course we have been down in the last five years, a few times, just for the weekend. My husband is a very busy man.

Mrs Aldridge Ah, that explains it. I'm never here at weekends. Mondays and Fridays, they're me days, one till three. Well it's supposed to be till three, but by the time we've had a cup of tea and a natter it's often nearer five.

Mavis A cup of tea and a natter!

Mrs Aldridge With your mum. We get on like a house on fire, your mum and me.

Mavis Oh nice. (*To Myra*) Mother obviously hasn't improved with age.

Myra I'm afraid not.

Mavis Where is she, by the way?

Myra Upstairs, getting dressed.

Mavis I suppose I had better go up and let her know I am here.

Mavis exits L

Mrs Aldridge finishes her glass of sherry

Mrs Aldridge Nice drop of sherry that. Nice glass too. Pity it's so small.

Myra I'm sorry, Mrs Aldridge. Would you like a *little* more?

Myra half fills the glass. Mrs Aldridge holds it out determinedly until it is filled

Mrs Aldridge Cheers.

Mavis comes back

Myra remains by the sideboard, clutching the bottle

Mavis Mother wouldn't let me in! She has locked her door and told me to wait downstairs. She says she will come down when she is ready.

Myra Mother is behaving most oddly. I offered to help her dress and she sent me away too.

Mrs Aldridge A very independent lady your mum. Aren't you going to offer your sister a drink, Mrs Carstairs? She looks as if she needs it.

Myra Would you like a sherry, Mavis?

Mavis Oh well, just a little one, as it is a celebration.

Myra I took the liberty of bringing a bottle in as I was sure Mother wouldn't have thought of it.

Mrs Aldridge chokes on her drink

Mavis (*grimly*) To the blushing bride. (*She sits on the settee* DL)

Mrs Aldridge Is your husband with you, Mrs — um — er?

Mavis Mrs Burton.

Myra (*sitting* UR) Yes, where is Gerald?

Mavis Ah, well, he thought there would be quite enough of a crowd here, so he dropped me off and said he would meet us at the Registrar's.

Myra But where is he now?

Mrs Aldridge In the pub if he's got any sense.

Myra Do you mind!

Mavis Well actually he did say he would go into the *George*, just for a coffee. He didn't want to sit in the car for half an hour.

Myra He should have come in.

Mavis Anyway, where is Kenneth? He's not here either.

Mrs Aldridge Perhaps he's in the *George* an' all.

Myra Mrs Aldridge, do you mind! Kenneth has gone to the Registrar's. We telephoned this morning, just to check the arrangements and there seemed to be some sort of mix-up, so Kenneth has gone to sort it out. He'll meet us there.

Mavis I see. So what are the arrangements. Who else is coming?

Myra Just Auntie Flo.

Mavis Is that all?

Myra Yes.

Mavis Not much of a wedding is it. And to think I spent forty pounds on this hat.

Myra Forty pounds! On a hat!

Mavis Yes.

Myra For Mother's wedding!

Mavis Well not exactly. I bought it for Gerald's niece's wedding last summer, but she broke off the engagement so I never wore it. I thought I might as well make use of it for Mother's wedding, even if it is only at a registry office.

Mavis takes off her hat. Myra comes across and picks it up

Myra Forty pounds! Gerald must be made of money.

Mavis Don't try to kid me you and Kenneth are short of a penny or two.

Myra Well I certainly wouldn't spend forty pounds on a hat.

Mavis So I see.

Mavis takes the hat from Myra and puts it on the seat beside her.
Myra meanwhile admires her own hat in the mirror

Mrs Aldridge I think your hat is very nice Mrs Carstairs. C & A
   isn't it?

Myra glares at Mrs Aldridge

   I thought I recognized it. My sister had one just like it for her
   Sharon's wedding. I got mine in the Oxfam shop, £1.50. Nice
   isn't it? I wore it for Sharon's wedding ... and the christening.

Mavis Very nice, Mrs Aldridge. Now Myra, to get back to
   Mother's wedding — so there's just us, Gerald and Kenneth
   and Auntie Flo. IsAuntie Flo coming here or going straight to
   the registry office?

Myra She is supposed to be coming here, but you know Auntie
   Flo.

Mavis Yes, only too well. And Mother and Ricardo. "Ricardo",
   what a name!

Myra And Ricardo's best man presumably.

Mavis That makes nine. Who is the best man?

Myra (*grimly*) One of the *other* waiters from the restaurant I
   suppose.

Mavis It gets worse and worse. I suppose you have met Ricardo,
   Myra. What is he like?

Mrs Aldridge Ooh, he's lovely. Ever so handsome.

Mavis Is he?

Myra It's a matter of taste.

   Mother enters L, *wearing a dressing -gown*

Mother What's a matter of taste?

Myra Mother, I thought you were getting dressed?

Mother I am.

Mavis Mother?

Mother Oh, hello Mavis.

Myra Mother, do go and get dressed. You don't want to be late for your own wedding, do you?

Mother Don't panic, Myra, there's no fear of that. I just came down to get myself a drink. (*She heads for the kitchen*) What is that you are drinking, Lily?

Myra It's sherry, sweet sherry. I brought it. Would you like a little sherry, Mother?

Mother Sweet sherry! Yuk, no thanks. A stiff whiskey is what I need.

Mavis Whiskey! Mother really, whatever next?

Myra (*pouring sherry and offering it to Mother*) Here you are, Mother, have a nice little sherry.

Mother No thank you, dear. I'll get my own drink.

Mother exits R

Myra Really, Mother gets more and more impossible. Now what am I going to do with this sherry now I've poured it? It's such a waste.

Mrs Aldridge Here, allow me. (*She grabs the sherry and returns to her seat*)

Myra returns to her seat. Mavis looks at her watch

Mavis What time are we due at the registry office?

Myra I said we would be there by twenty past.

Mavis What about Auntie Flo?

Myra What about her?

Mavis Shouldn't she be here by now?

Myra Oh, yes, I suppose so.

Mavis Oughtn't we to do something about it?

Myra Do what?

Mavis I don't know. Go and look for her. You know how absent-minded she is.

Myra I haven't got time to go chasing round looking for Auntie Flo.

Mrs Aldridge Shall I go?

Mavis What good would that do. You don't even know her, do you?

Mrs Aldridge 'Course I do. She's your mum's old auntie. She's been here lots of times. She comes on the twenty three bus, or the nineteen if she's changed at the market. I'll walk up to the bus stop.

Myra Would you Mrs Aldridge. That would be most kind of you.

Mrs Aldridge No trouble. I needed a smoke anyway, and I know your mum don't like it.

Mrs Aldridge exits L

Mavis Whatever possessed Mother to invite her charlady to her wedding. I thought we had agreed it would be a very small affair, strictly family only.

Myra Mother insisted. Mind you, as I told you on the phone, if Mother had had her way it would have been a grand wedding with half a dozen of her old cronies as bridesmaids and a reception for about a hundred. Thank goodness I talked her out of that.

Mavis It's a pity you couldn't talk her out of re-marrying at all.

Myra I tried. Believe me, I tried.

Mavis It's all so embarrassing. Who is this Ricardo she's marrying? What do we know about him? Where did she meet him?

Myra Well, Mother doesn't tell me everything as you well know,

but as far as I can make out he is a waiter from an Italian
restuarant in the town centre. It opened about a year ago and
Mother started going in there for coffee, well it's handy, right
next door to *Sainsbury's* and opposite the bus stop. Anyway,
apparently one day there was some sort of panic in the kitchen
— the chef had fallen and broken his arm, or something — so
Mother rolled up her sleeves and waded in to help. She was
invited to a slap up dinner as a thank you, and it all grew from
that. The first I knew about it was when Mother announced she
was getting married. Father must be turning in his grave.

Mavis (*groaning*) An Italian waiter. Oh God, he will be our
stepfather!

Myra I know.

Mavis I don't think I can bear it. An Italian waiter! I suppose he
is Italian. It would be even worse if he was a cockney putting
on a phoney Italian accent to make the place seem authentic.

Myra Oh he's Italian all right. Comes from Milan, or is it Turin?

Mother enters R *carrying a large, much decorated glass of
Pimms*

Mother Naples, actually.

Myra (*leaping up*) Mother! Whatever have you got there? That
isn't whiskey ——

Mother No, I decided I just fancied a Pimms. Cheers. Ah, lovely.
Just right. (*She sits* UR) Where's Lily?

Mavis Lily?

Mother Mrs Aldridge.

Myra She's gone to the bus stop to look for Auntie Flo.

Mother Has she? Poor old Flo. You really shouldn't have asked
her to come. It's not worth it for the paltry little "do" you're
insisting on having. Now if I'd had my way, we'd have a proper
wedding with the reception at Ricardo's, then it really would

have been worth while. Still, that's your loss. I must get
dressed.

Mother exits L

Mavis I suppose she is right in a way. After all it is her wedding.

Myra Mavis, can you imagine the embarrassment of it all. It's
all right for you, you don't live here anymore, but Kenneth and
I would never be able to hold our heads up in this town again.
If Mother insists on making a fool of herself the best we can do
is to keep it as quiet as possible. Just a small family ceremony
and then Kenneth has booked a table for lunch at the *Mitre*, just
for the eight of us.

Mavis Why the *Mitre*?

Myra It's quieter than the *George*, and we are not likely to meet
anyone we know there.

Mavis That's for sure! A table for eight, did you say? I thought
there were nine of us.

Myra Oh, we didn't include Mrs Aldridge. I told her it was just
family. She quite understood. She seemed quite pleased actually. (*She picks up Mavis's hat*) Did you really pay forty pounds
for this? Can I try it on? (*She takes off her own hat and tries
Mavis's, looking in the mirror*) Hmm. Can't say it does
anything for me. Just as well. I couldn't bring myself to pay that
sort of money just for a hat.

Mavis (*taking the hat from her and putting it back on the seat*)
We all have our priorities.

Mrs Aldridge enters L

Mrs Aldridge No sign of your Auntie Flo, I'm afraid. I waited for
the twenty- three and the nineteen but she wasn't on either of
them.

Myra Oh dear, she has probably forgotten all about it. Thank you anyway, Mrs Aldridge.

Mrs Aldridge stands by the sherry bottle and coughs loudly

Oh do help yourself to another sherry, Mrs Aldridge, if you really must.

Mrs Aldridge Well I think I deserve it. (*She pours herself a sherry and returns to her seat* DR) Cheers. Hasn't your mum come down yet?

Mavis She ought to be ready by now, it's time we were leaving. (*She goes to the door* L *and shouts*) Mother, you are going to be late for your wedding.

Mother enters and sweeps to C

Mother No I won't. And there's no need to shout.

Myra Mother! Whatever are you wearing!

Mavis You can't get married dressed like that.

Mother Why not? There's no law against it is there?

Mavis But Mother — trousers!

Myra And that hat!

Mavis And those shoes!

Mrs Aldridge I think you look very nice.

Mother Thank you, Lily.

Mrs Aldridge Very suitable for the occasion if you don't mind me saying so.

Myra Mother, I absolutely insist that you go and change. That outfit is completely unsuitable for a wedding. Wear the hat if you must, but not the trousers, definitely *not* the trousers.

Mother I'm sorry you don't like the trousers. I like them. So does Ricardo. And the hat. In fact Ricardo chose the hat.

Mavis Ricardo chose the hat?

Mother Yes, when we were staying in Eastbourne.

Mavis (*shocked*) You went to Eastbourne with Ricardo?

Myra You told me you were going with the Mother's Union.

Mother Oh I did go with the Mother's Union. Ricardo met me there.

Myra You mean he was there all week!

Mother No dear, not all week. He had to come back for a couple of days to sort out some things at the restaurant. Business things you know.

Mavis I thought he was only a waiter.

Mother Who told you that?

Mavis Myra did.

Mother Yes, she would. No dear, he is not a waiter, he owns the restaurant, or at least he did own it. He's just sold it. Got a very good price for it too. That's why he had to come back from Eastbourne, to sign the contract.

Mavis (*crossing to Myra*) Why did you tell me he was just a waiter?

Myra Oh never mind that now. Whatever he is, he'll be standing outside the registrar's office and Mother is going to be late, so will you please go and change, you cannot get married dressed like that.

Mother Oh I quite agree, dear.

Myra Then will you please ...

Mother (*sitting* DL) But then, I'm not getting married.

Mavis You're not getting married. What a relief!

Mother No dear, I'm already married. Ricardo and I got married by special licence, at Eastbourne.

Myra You can't have.

Mother Oh, but we have.

Myra But what about today — the registrar's office — lunch at the *Mitre* — it's all booked — Kenneth and Gerald are waiting ...

Mother That's your problem, Myra dear, not mine. Ricardo and

I wanted a nice big wedding with all our friends there. A jolly
party at the restaurant afterwards, with champagne, and a big
wedding cake, and a band for dancing. (*She gets up*) But no, that
didn't suit my stuck-up daughters did it. You didn't approve of
such a carry-on did you. So you made me cancel all my plans
and you organized this hole-in-the-corner affair, with only the
closest family present to witness my undesirable and degrading
marriage to an Italian waiter! You tried to make Ricardo and me
feel ashamed because, at our age, we are in love, and happy, and
we wanted all our friends to be happy with us. Well, we are not
ashamed and we want nothing whatsoever to do with your
grubby little wedding arrangements, so there!

Myra But Mother ...

Mother (*pushing past her and moving* R) So Ricardo and I made
our own arrangements. We got married a month ago, and today,
while you are having your dreary little lunch at the *Mitre* ... the
MITRE! ... you couldn't even bring yourselves to take us to the
George! Well, we shall be on our way to Italy. First Class. Oh
you might as well go ahead and have your lunch, Ricardo has
insisted on paying for it. He's even ordered champagne, though
heaven knows you don't deserve it.

Mavis (*crossing to Mother*) Mother, please stop this. Come and
sit down.

Mother (*sitting* UR) Poor Mavis, poor both of you. I don't know
how I managed to have two such miserable daughters, without
a scrap of warmth or humour between you. Well yes, I do know,
you're like your father, God rest his soul. I was never good
enough for him; well I should never have married him. I was a
great disappointment. Still, you two made up for it. Oh he was
proud of you.

Myra How can you speak of Father like that.

Mother Ricardo's just the opposite, you see. He's warm and
funny and loving, and he thinks I'm the bee's knees.

Mavis Don't be such a fool, Mother. He's after your money.

Mother After my money? Why Mavis, whatever gave you that idea? Ricardo has pots of money. He has restaurants all over the place. We could live anywhere, but he wants to go back to Italy before he's too old. Oh, he's got restaurants there too. (*Gloating*) I don't know whether we'll keep the rest of the British ones, or the one in Paris. We'll just have to see.

Myra Mother, are you trying to tell us that you are going to Italy to live?

Mother Yes.

Mavis But Mother you can't. You don't speak the language.

Mother I'm not too old to learn. In fact I'm already learning. (*She speaks a few words in Italian*)

Mrs Aldridge applauds

Myra But what about this house, everything here ...?

Mother (*getting up*) Ah yes. (*She takes some keys from her pocket*) The house is let for a year. I've done it through an agency. They will deal with all the finances, so there is no need for you to bother your pretty little heads. Lily here will be in charge. (*She hands Mrs Aldridge the keys*) She will see that the place is kept clean and in good order, so get in touch with her if you have any queries. After the year is up we'll decide what to do with it. We may sell it, we may keep it for holidays, who can tell.

Car horn sounds outside

Ah, that will be Ricardo. (*She crosses to collect her bag* L)

Mrs Aldridge (*going towards the door* L) I'll come and see you off. (*To the girls*) I'll come back and lock up when you're ready to go.

Mother Well girls, are you going to wish me luck? (*She kisses* *them both and moves towards the door* L)

Myra But the registrar's — Kenneth's waiting ...

Mother Oh we cancelled all that weeks ago. Your Kenneth is wasting his time... Oh, just one other thing ... Ricardo picked up Auntie Flo on his way here. I was going to put her off, but it seemed a shame to do the poor old thing out of a free lunch. (*Putting on a pair of sunglasses*) *Ciao!*

Mother exits L *with Mrs Aldridge*

Mavis and Myra stare after them

Myra But Mother ...

Auntie Flo enters

Flo Hello Myra, hello Mavis. (*She sits on Myra's hat on the settee*) How kind of you to ask me to lunch.

Mavis Oh no! My hat! (*She rescues it*) Forty pounds that cost!

CURTAIN

FURNITURE AND PROPERTY LIST

Only essential furniture and properties are listed here. Further dressing may be added at the Director's discretion

On stage:	Small settee. *Beside it:* **Mother's** bag
	Two easy chairs
	Small table
	Sideboard. *On it:* sherry bottle, glasses.
	Over it: mirror
Off stage:	Large decorated glass of Pimms **(Mother)**
	Keys **(Mother)**
Personal:	**Mavis:** watch
	Mother: sunglasses

LIGHTING PLOT

Property fittings required: nil
Interior. The same scene throughout

To open: General interior lighting

No cues

EFFECTS PLOT

Cue 1 **Mrs Aldridge:** "... I'd die..."   (Page 2)
     Doorbell

Cue 2 **Mother:** "... who can tell."   (Page 14)
     Car horn